The Official Study Guide

Tuning In to
God's Call

*Andrew Carl Wisdom, OP
and Christine Kiley, ASCJ*

NEW PRIORY PRESS

EXPLORING THE DOMINICAN VISION

Cover photo adapted from the cover of *Tuning In to God's Call* (*Liguori*, 2012)
Production Editor: Terry L. Jarbe

ISBN-13: 978-1623110468

Dedication

To Christine Hallett, Carla Vaughan, and Barbara Wisdom:
My sisters, who are eloquent examples of how to live one's life *tuned in to God's call*.

~Fr. Andrew Carl Wisdom, O.P.

Dedicated to my Sisters - Apostles of the Sacred Heart of Jesus in our Clelian Heights community, and to High School religion teachers and friends who teach *God's Call* with love. After using *Tuning In to God's Call* in class, they were the inspiration to provide the Study Guide.

~Sr. Christine Kiley, A.S.C.J.

Contents

About Using This Study Guide

This Study Guide can be used in a variety of ways:
- For group sessions led by Campus Ministers to assist discerning young adults on college campuses
- For high school teachers in Religion LIFE CHOICES courses
- By individuals discerning alone or with spiritual guides or in groups with vocation directors
- Evangelization groups and Youth Groups in parishes

As you follow the steps laid out in this workbook, you will learn how the process of discernment can help you recognize and name the signs of God's plan for your life. God desires that we come to understand His Word and His daily call in our lives. This study guide is designed to help you to explore more fully and commit to integrating the values expressed in its companion book **TUNING IN TO GOD'S CALL**. Its purpose is to further clarify and solidify the insights gained in **TUNING IN TO GOD'S CALL** as you work through all five stages of discernment through practical application.

Therefore you will need a copy of *TUNING IN TO GOD'S CALL with you as the essential resour*ce to accompany this workbook. It will be helpful to re-read sections of the book in order to answer the questions from specific passages in the book. Each passage points to qualities and important stages in the discernment process. By reading the Scripture Quote, Reflection, Saint Quote and Prayer provided on each page you will then be prepared to respond to the questions posed in each section of the study guide. Utilizing the study guide with the book will offer the best opportunity of an effective and comprehensive discernment. A successful discernment is one that leads to a decision.

OVERVIEW of AUTHORS' APPROACH
to STUDY GUIDE

INTRODUCTION OF STAGES

PART I	**What is Discernment?**
PART II	**Why Should a Person Discern?**
PART III	**How Does One Begin Discerning?**
PART IV	**How Does Discernment Lead to Action?**
PART V	**Signs of a Good Discernment.**

Each of the five stages is an overview and will have specific questions, discussion prompts and prayers. The format will vary according to the interest, age and approach of those discerning and can be covered alone, in prayer or with a discussion group.

PART I
What is Discernment?

In the original book Tuning In to God's Call, read the section: What is Discernment? P. 13

1. Begin by quietly reading the prayer of St. Catherine of Siena. Do you identify with her prayer? If so how? What does Catherine tell us about desire?

2. Since desires play an important part in discernment, can you now name some desires? In your heart? Are you able to name your desires as Catherine was? What is the difference between say, the desire for a particular GPA or an updated iPhone and those deeper desires hidden in the depth of our hearts?

3. What did you think discernment meant before reading this book? In your own words put what you think it means. (Try to do this without looking at the book.)

4. This section points out that "we are called to be the Lord's instruments in the world." Can you recall a time when you felt you were God's instrument in a situation? What and how does God's call to us have anything to do with our personal discernment?

5. In what special response to that call do you think you would most flourish? What do the authors mean when they make the point that we are not here to survive—we are not here to simply live ---we are here to thrive?

6. Our generous gift of sharing our lives may leave us pondering many different life calls. Which life call most appeals to you at this moment of the four vocational choices mentioned in this section?

WAKING UP

Something woke you up or you would not be reading this study guide now.

1. Can you trace the fingerprints of God in your vocational awakening?

2. What do you have to do to stay awake and "tuned in"? WHO helps you to stay tuned in?

3. Our parents had their own way of waking us up again and again. List God's favorite ways of waking you up again and again to a potential vocation.

4. What is "the more" that God is waking up in you?

5. What makes you spiritually drowsy in your discernment efforts?

6. Like the coworkers in this reflection have you wondered, "What is the meaning of my life?"

7. List the obstacles to maintaining a wakefulness to the tone and tenor of God's voice.

8. Write a brief letter to God about your desire to be truly open to Him.

ADSUM

1. In the ADSUM reflection, Mary had fewer questions to ask Gabriel (who appeared with a message for Mary from God) than most discerners. The Biblical passage indicates that Mary asked one question: How can this be… since I know not man?

2. Have you ever taken the same question to God: "How can this be? I am too young; I love my friends, my job, and my income?" Are YOU honestly open to God's answer?

3. Can you frame in your heart some other responses to the question of Gabriel? How are you willing to serve God? Are you completely available to anyone or to do any service asked for others?

4. How does the thought of service, responding to God's call, stretch you beyond your comfort zone? What feelings surface?

5. Take this response ADSUM to prayer and spend time with Mary asking questions, imagining the future.

Record your responses and remember it is ok to express shock or surprise. My first response was "NOT ME! NEVER ME! Not me God, not now!" God meets us where we are, not where we think we should be.

DISCERNMENT

1. What is the place of PEACE that many hope for?

2. Can you name what the place of peace feels like, looks like? For you? Consider times, places, circumstances where you have felt most peaceful. What preceded that sense of peace?

3. In order to weigh your options it is helpful to approach the questions with a process. Consider any choice---job, college, and project and list the pros and cons of this question:

      PROS

      CONS

4. Remember all choices will have some aspects that appear positive, some negative. In consideration, which of them brings you the most joy?

5. Do you find openness difficult?

6. Try to be open with a trusted friend or relative regarding possible responses to the two sides of your choice. Remember this can be any choice – not necessarily your major life, vocational choice. Circle which of the pros and cons listed earlier most reflect you at this time.

THE THREE CALLS

1. Connie had a lightning bolt experience. Have you ever been shocked to experience an unexpected bright thought of sudden clarity seemingly "out of the blue?" Journal about this experience.

2. Often we hear the phrase in conversations with people, "a tug on your heart." This phrase can mean a haunting and never ending question that continues to repeat itself for a long time. Are you able to name some grace-filled inspirations, "tugs of the heart," in your thinking, in your prayer and in your heart? Sensitive pondering? Caring friend? Unexpected openness?

3. Examine the list below and check the qualities that are clearly identifiable in your life right now. Try to check them as spontaneously as possible while pondering them.

___peace and calm
___joyful freedom
___meekness and gentleness
___openness to others
___cooperative spirit
___faithfulness to promises
___trust in a plan
___patience
___kindness
___generous thoughts

These qualities are God-like characteristics that can assist you in responding to grace-filled inspirations, tugs of the heart, on the way to discovering your life's calling.

BUILDING OUR SPIRITUAL MUSCLES

The goal of building our spiritual muscles is to become a fit, strong *athlete of Christ.*

1. How do you "practice love," "exercise your faith," and "work out hope" to keep in good spiritual shape?

2. Are you one who typically perseveres in something or procrastinates? Where is perseverance called for to further your discernment at this point in your life?

3. What burden or sin clings to you that gets in the way of the race of faith?

4. Which muscle would move your discernment forward if it were further developed? Faith? Hope? Or love?

5. How do you build your spiritual muscles? What approach do you most frequently use to exercise your soul?

6. Create a personalized training program to allow you to get into the best spiritual shape possible to discern effectively. (How many sets, repetitions and exercises a day would you plan?)

7. Since love is a decision and commitment, when do you feel that love and the call to live your faith most challenges and stretches you?

LIVING LIFE TO THE FULLEST

Consider and list the people that you admire who have lived full and challenging lives.

1. Name what qualities and virtues drew you to these people.

2. What gifts of life did they exhibit that inspired you?

3. Did you ever realize that God wants everyone to experience truth, beauty, goodness and all of the fullness a life has to offer?

4. What is your immediate reaction to what Jesus said in the Gospel: "I have come that you may have life and have it to the full"?

5. What would "fullness of life" look like to you?

COME FOR THE RIDE

Some of the bumps in the road of life could be:
- Pleasure
- Possessions
- Desire to be recognized

1. How could these values or desires prevent you from seeing the plan of God for your life?

2. Have you ever considered that God's desire for you and the deepest longings of your heart might be saying the same thing? God speaks to us in and through the whispers of our hearts.

3. Can you name the values that may assist you in seeing the plan of God for your life?

4. God will assist you in directing your life toward the good—however it may not always be clear or immediate. Uncertainty could be a part of the plan of life. Have you experienced uncertainty in your discernment? Can you name where it started? Is it consistent?

CAREER OR CALL?

Our education, family and culture dictate some of our choices. Perhaps we can now look at some life choices.

- Call
  1. Marriage
  2. Intentional Single life
  3. Priesthood
  4. Consecrated Life

- Career
  5. Health Care
  6. Accounting/Finance
  7. Business
  8. Education
  9. Therapy

1. Can you add some choices to each list?

2. Why do many people think that all 1-9 are careers?

3. **On a scale of 1 to 10**: Each particular call to love brings with it great joy as well as moments of great challenge…can you consider what some of those might be?

Least   Most
appealing 1...2...3...4...5...6...7...8...9...10 appealing

Circle the options under call that began this section above that are most appealing. Assign a number value next to them utilizing the scale above.

4. Reflect upon this issue: What would challenge you the most in the married life? In the single life? In the priesthood or consecrated life?

BE ON THE LOOKOUT FOR GOD

1. What is Alex's basic approach to God? How does he relate to God? What have you learned from his attitude?

2. Why was Alex confident that he was in Heaven and God was to be found there? Where is your confidence in faith in those who have told you where God can be found?

3. How, like Alex, can you daily be on "the look-out for God?" What are some of the different ways? Note the ways below. (Sketch a concept-mapping diagram)

4. Do you see yourself as "working" for God?

5. In what calling, although it may hold challenges, would you most flourish?

6. What does that look like now? What could that look like in the future?

7. What are the clues of how God already uses you as His "co-worker?"

PART II

Why Should One Discern?

In the original book Tuning In to God's Call, read the section: Why should one discern? p. 36

1. In a spirit of prayer and faith seeking to know God's will for you----begin this journey in trust and with a peaceful spirit. In your own words, do you understand why discernment is an important process?

2. What might some of the issues with trust be, especially for a young adult in today's world?

3. What do you believe is the most vital reason to discern? As you move forward you may feel God visit you with His grace. Remain open and receptive and record the "visits" as best you can. What might be the benefit of "seeing more clearly?" What might be the fears?

4. It is hoped that the process of discernment will summon you to grow. Have you been able to see and own that growth?

5. Can you name some clear designs---that is some messages or signs---that God has shown you in your childhood, your teenage years, your young adult years? Do these patterns assist you in seeing that God has been a part of your growth?

COMMITTING TO GOD'S DESIGN

1. Brainstorm what comes immediately to mind when you hear the word, "saint."

2. How do you define "sanctity?"

3. Are you truly open to God's design for you to be a saint?

4. How would someone become struck in their own life plans?

5. Pause in honest reflection: in your recent week, in your daily walk with God, did you adhere to the path of God's design or did you detour to your own? How will the direction you are traveling in help you or assist you to make positive choices for your life?

6. As you go about your daily life, is your gaze on yourself or God?

LIVING IN THE PRESENT:

1. Before you read this book, what did you think was the *unum necessarium*, "the one thing necessary?"

2. Who do your most readily identify with, Martha or Mary?

3. If Martha, what are the things you are most anxious about? Make a list.

4. What most robs you of the better part that Mary experiences, the *unum necessarium*?

5. What circumstances in your life could be keeping you from living a more spiritual existence?

6. What would bring more focus to your life?

7. As the old song goes, we can "look for love in all the wrong places." What are those places for you?

8. What absorbs you in the past and worries you about the future?

DARE TO COMMIT

1. What thoughts go through your head when you hear the word "commitment?"

2. Can you name the most committed person that you know? What were their qualities or characteristics?

3. Do you struggle to believe that you can fall in love and then commit to that love?

HOLINESS

1. The call to holiness includes all Christians whatever their state of life: Agree/Disagreed? Comment:

2. In what ways do you recognize holiness?

3. In a culture that says "if it feels good, do it," how can one be holy without being countercultural?

SURRENDER

1. What does the landscape of your life look like? What do the brushstrokes tell you?

2. What needs to be filled in on the canvas?

3. Measure where you are at on the scale of committed involvement in owning your Christian discipleship: The top of the ladder is the freedom of boundless love. The middle is mediocrity. The bottom is paralysis "in my Christian witness."

FOLLOW CHRIST

1. Name a time when you did what you knew you had to do because you felt called to it.

2. What surprised you about Fr. Giles' story? What was the price of his sacrifice?

3. How have you exercised the "discipline of love" in your life?

4. In what situations did you avoid its price?

GOD PERFECTS ME

1. Do you suffer from a fear of or obsession with perfectionism?

2. Can you see the radical movements in our world today? What are positive? What are negative?

3. What is radical in your Christian witness?

4. What is your role in "God's perfecting of you?" Comment.

Part III
How Does One Begin Discerning?

In the original book Tuning In to God's Call, read the section: How Does One Begin Discerning? p. 52

1. Are there people in my life with whom I can be present that make a difference in their understanding of my walk with God? How does their presence affect my life choices?

2. It takes great attention to be present to others. Presence to others helps one with presence to God's movements in my life. How is this evident in my own life?

3. How does God relate to me and call me into relationship? When I am present to God, what feelings, thoughts and emotions can be named?

4. Are there practices in your present situation that assist you in getting in touch with your God-moments? Jesus wanted his disciples to be in touch with God's presence by listening to His words---in life, in prayer, in scripture. What are the best ways that you feel you are in touch with God? How do you listen?

5. Do I know, and can I name, the pattern of God's love in my life? Have you considered discussing these indicators of God's love in your life… with a trusted friend, a spiritual director or a confessor?

6. Is there anything about what you are feeling, perceiving or experiencing that you are hesitant to name or talk about? Why do you think there is a hesitancy?

MARITAL LOVE

1. Is marriage a vocation, a "calling"? Explain.

2. How do the Catholic Bishops describe marital commitment?

3. Is marriage primarily for the two people in love?

4. How does a man or woman lead each other to Christ through marriage? List the possible ways.

5. What image does marriage reflect? What relationship does it mirror?

BRINGING PEOPLE TO CHRIST

1. If someone asked you the same question Fr. Wisdom's brother, Larry, asked him, what would be your response?

2. What is the impetus or motivation for Christian discipleship?

3. What do we mean when we say the Church is *apostolic*? How does this impact your own following of Christ as a member of the Church?

4. Have you ever experienced bringing someone to Christ like St. Andrew? Or someone bring you closer to Christ?

5. What is the true longing and desire for which your heart is waiting for?

6. Name some ways that you can bring others to Christ.

PAY IT FORWARD

1. St. Ignatius's challenge is to imagine yourself at the end of your life. What moments of your life would you be most proud and happy to remember when your last day on earth is approaching? What choices?

2. Take a sneak peek at your future. What do you want it to look like?

3. What would you wish to have chosen at life's end considering the choices you have made?

4. How do you want people to remember you? Write your own eulogy.

IS GOD ENOUGH?

1. Have you taken on this question like Vince and wrestled with it for your own life?

2. God "broke in" on Vince's agenda. Have you ever sensed that He interrupted your life and agenda as well?

3. Do you find it difficult to trust in God's map for your life? Why?

4. What would it take for you to believe St. Paul's words that God's grace is enough for you?

GOT PASSION?

1. Do you agree with Cardinal Dolan's statement about Christ being the passion of our lives? Is that passion primary in your own life?

2. What does "holy zeal" look like in your life?

3. Can you name some of the people who have served as your mentors or models in zeal and passion?

4. Examine the level of zeal and passion in your own life. How can you concretely deepen both?

A UNIQUE MISSION

1. Have you had an early experience in your life that profoundly sharped your worldview like Father Wisdom did?

2. Has anyone told you that you have a special mission in life that only you can fill?

3. What has been the catalyst in your search for your life's mission?

4. Have you ever feared missing God's plan for your life?

RUN TO WIN

1. What have been the toughest miles for you in running the road of discernment?

2. Describe the peaks. Describe the valleys.

3. Name ways you most effectively exercise the spiritual muscles of faith, hope and love.

4. What tools are you *not* utilizing?

5. Have you ever experienced the inner authority of another?
Has someone ever "followed you" because of your inner authority?

6. What one effort today would further your discernment?

TRANSFORM THE WORLD

1. What do we mean by sacrament?

2. How do you understand the sacramental nature and purpose of marriage?

3. What would you positively bring to marriage?

4. What habits would you have to change to avoid approaching it as: "what I can get out of it for myself?"

JOYFUL PRESENCE

1. Is joy essential or just a nice trait in a Christian? If essential, why?

2. What are instances of joy or humor that you have experienced in your faith?

3. At this point in your life, is your joy or humor a part of your Christian witness?

Part IV
How Does Discernment
Lead to Action?

In the original book Tuning In to God's Call, read the section: Does Discernment Lead to Action? P. 74

1. "There is not a moment in which God does not present Himself under the cover of some pain to be endured, of some consolation to be enjoyed, or of some duty to be performed. All that takes place within us, around us, or through us, contains and conceals His divine action. We do not recognize his operation until it has passed us by. If we watched with vigilant attention God would endlessly reveal himself to us and we should exclaim: 'It is the Lord!'"

~Jean-Pierre de Caussade

React to de Caussade's reflection. How do his words speak to your experience?

2. At this point, since you have been praying and trying to be spiritually attentive, you may be consciously blessed with God revealing himself through people, places, and events. If so, take a moment to journal about them. Be concrete in your examples.

• • •

3. Spend some time praying with these instances of divine revelations that you have been journaling about. Sometimes the Lord works so very gradually that you may not have recognized these occurrences of God's revelations. With prayerful gratitude, journal and pray to the Lord asking that He reveal Himself further to you whether in a still small voice, in a nature scene, in a conversation, in a book or movie…

4. Keep in mind as you move toward a decision that those who have gone before you and have made the leap of faith have also had fears and doubts, but have placed their trust in our God who is faithful. How connected do you feel to others who have gone before you on this journey of discernment? What does God's faithfulness look like to you?

5. Do you feel you have explored the choices with prayer and peaceful study of the alternatives? If so, how? If not, what more do you need to do?

FORGETTING OURSELVES ON PURPOSE

1. There are some qualities for authentic discernment that are critical—openness, generosity and courage to name a few. To make a conscious decision to "forget oneself on purpose" will require what thinking and what doing on the part of the discerner? Hint—reflect on the attitude of Christ. (Phil 2: 5-7)

2. In a culture of individualism, materialism, and hedonism how does a person make choices on a regular basis to forget oneself on purpose?

3. Is it possible to moderate the activities, pleasures and pressures of life to be a discerning person? What does that look like for you?

4. How will the group of friends with whom you belong be able to deal with your risking to live the new ambition of forgetting yourself on purpose? Name any fears that come to mind.

5. "The desire for God is written in the human heart… and God never ceases to draw man to himself" (CCC 27). God's desire for living His life and call in us is the very making of a person who "forgets self." How can one go about blending God's desire with one's own agenda and plans? Are they even compatible?

READY FOR THE PLUNGE

1. Transitions are never easy. What are some of the ways God can stretch us during a time of transition? How has He stretched you? What leaps of faith has He asked you to make?

2. How can immersion in the culture of religious life/priesthood assist you in discerning?

3. Where have you grown in maturity and self-knowledge through this process?

4. Openness to the Divine Call will evoke probing questions -- ponder the most difficult and heartfelt questions for you.

5. Letting go is a generous act of self-giving, but it could open doors to confusion, questions, fears and uncertainty. Which "door" is the most difficult for you?

6. How willing or reluctant are you to let go and take the plunge so that God's plan can help you move forward?

WASTING TIME WITH GOD

1. The eleven-year-old boy who heard his parents talking found his own definition of contemplative prayer. What do you think of the boy's definition? What would be your own? Write it down.

2. In your life where do you experience inner peace, spiritual joy and elevation of your mind to God and spiritual things?

3. Is it comfortable or difficult for you to "waste time with God?" Is it productive?

4. When in love, it is common to sit for hours and just chat or sit without words in someone's company? How often do I find myself in this posture with God?

5. From what you have read in this reflection, how does prayer progress?

LISTEN WITH YOUR HEART

1. When you don't concentrate "your listening" from your heart or any particular place, where naturally do you listen from? From your head? From your fears? From your sense of self-worth or what others might think?

2. When you do listen with your heart, that place of pure love and deep freedom away from your fears, what does it tell you?

3. What does it mean to listen with your "spiritual ear"? What do you hear when you do? What is your "default" listening?

4. Give examples from Scriptures where people listened well and where they clearly were not listening well.

5. List what your mind plays incessantly when you are not in control of the conversation in your head.

6. What do you have to do to shift your ability to hear Christ's voice rather than all the other voices competing for your attention?

7. Spiritually, listening with your heart, what do you hear when the words "Follow Me!" are spoken?

OPEN THE DOOR

1. Each day is a blessed new beginning. What are some practical ways to open the door to God's new blessings each morning?

2. Resolutions can come and go. What is the one resolution that this reflection suggests that you include in your prayer life this year? How are you instructed to be faithful to it?

3. Sometimes we slam the door on God when we are upset or angry with Him. To reopen that door, what would you say if He were sitting across from your kitchen table today? Describe the conversation.

4. Spiritual masters consistently recommend that if you need to forfeit any section of your prayer life—the one area to never neglect is the night *examen* (see Glossary of Terms) or reflection on the events of the day. Name where you were present to God and His blessings today. Note where you were not present to His graces.

LETTING CHRIST IN

1. What is the difference between *living* your life and *surviving* it?

2. Explain the distinction between living a life of *self-assertion* or a life of *self-donation*.

3. What are the things you would have to eliminate from your life to truly let Christ into your life?

4. List those people, things or cravings that crowd Christ out of your life.

5. What one thing can you do right now to welcome Christ into your heart?

THE VOICE WITHIN

1. How does our contemporary culture answer Pilate's question, "What is Truth?" What are the truths the world proposes?

2. How does a Christian define Truth?

3. How does the Triune God permeate your life and sustain your existence? How do your unique gifts bring service to your community?

4. Name those things that make you a good listener of God's voice.

5. What other voices, apart from God's, compete for your attention within? List them.

6. What suggestions would you have if someone asked you how to keep focused on the True Voice within?

MY LIFE IS NOT MY OWN

1. What are the two unhelpful myths with which we are often raised? Have you bought into these myths in your own life? What makes them "unhelpful?"

2. The desires of the human heart find rest in God's desires for the person. Jesus desired the heart of the rich young man. Like him, is there one thing lacking in your ability to be fully alive and truly happy?

3. All gifts merge into God's plan when we surrender to the plan of God in our hearts! Since we are naturally restless as human beings, what will it take for you to surrender and rest your heart in God?

4. In the Our Father, we pray, "Thy will be done." How can it be translated into modern thinking? Reword it to make it more poignant and meaningful for your discernment journey today.

5. What is the destiny of the gifts God gives you, especially the gift of your own life?

6. List the ways you can make a return to God for a small part of what He has given to you.

CLEARING AWAY THE CLUTTER

1. In order to be holy, do you have to become a completely different person?

2. What does Michelangelo's approach to art suggest about God's approach to making us holy?

3. Does God, the grand artist of all seen and unseen beauty, need our help in making us holy?

4. Where is holiness similar and where is it completely different?

5. Where is your focus spiritually? On all that you are not or on all that you are?

ALLOWING CHRIST TO ENTER YOUR LIFE

1. How does Christ most want to relate to you?

2. Describe your idea of friendship. Describe Christ's idea of friendship.

3. If the purpose of the Church is to call you to be more, what is "the more" that you are going to allow Christ to call you to this year? Why is that important?

4. Do you play small in your life? Have you been tempted toward spiritual mediocrity?

5. List the things you have to do to spiritually "get off the couch."

THE PRICE IS HIGH

1. Elizabeth took the high road. What enabled her to do so in the face of such painful opposition and obvious persecution?

2. It has been said that God only gives crosses that He knows a person can endure. Elizabeth seemed to have excessive obstacles to her call. What would you think or feel if you were in her position? How would you handle being so opposed?

3. God's grace brings us to a state of spiritual freedom. Is it reflected in Elizabeth's journey? How and where?

4. How could a discerning woman in Elizabeth's situation best express the stirrings within during this stage of her Tuning In to God's call? (Hint: Habakkuk 2:3).

5. Have you considered how high the price to follow Christ can be? Are you resolved to pay the cost or are you still struggling with its demands?

Part V
Signs of a Good Discernment

In the original book Tuning In to God's Call, read the section: What is Discernment? P. 94

1. With a small group, read together the common signs of a good discernment. In discussing it with others, you may find that each person in discernment had a variety of responses and that "their signs" were not "your signs" or simply came in a different order.

2. Having gathered information on the choices that you are considering and completing the "getting to know you" phase, it is a time when decisions for the future may be made. This process can take place over months or years. List some interest, attraction and desires that have consistently come into your life and relationship.

3. The reflection questions on page 95 of *Tuning In to God's Call* are very helpful at this stage of the process. Team up with another person and go through them together.

4. God usually blesses you with some certainty about your decision and an open sharing characterizes the divine movement toward a peace about the next step into the future. Has there been confirmation–that deep affirmation of heart that gives you some certitude that this is what God desires of you? Can you name, record or share these confirmations?

THE CALL CONFIRMED

1. Amelia had tasted many phases of adult life. After many great jobs and successful practice why was she searching for more? What was the MORE for which she was searching?

2. Searching does not always or immediately finalize a choice in the discerning of a life call. How deep into her past life did Amelia search before arriving at some clues of the MORE in her life?

3. In her decision to begin sharing her deep desires with people, what were some providential circumstances and reactions to Amelia's call? What were your thoughts about the people and their reactions to her life decisions?

4. Is it evident to you how or why Amelia was able to embrace her call?

5. Confirming signs are not always obvious in the discernment of a call in life. Why are prayer and discussion critical to the process? Can you understand why discernment cannot be successful when undertaken in a vacuum?

6. "The desire for God is written in the human heart and God never ceases to draw the human heart" (CCC27). How does this apply to Amelia? How does this apply to your own discernment?

THE PAINFUL YES

1. Is inner turmoil a usual occurrence in the discernment journey?

2. Everyone has emotions that can be triggered at any given moment. How can a person know if these emotions raise questions that lead to a decision or are obstacles to clarification? What did it do in Kelly's case?

3. Do these types of struggle help with deepening one's commitment? Answer from within your own story.

4. How did Kelly deal with her questions—could she have tried differently?

5. Can you think of some question that you were not sure how to handle? Did you not know where to turn or did you feel alone?

6. A crisis like this can be totally preoccupying. In the end what was Kelly's saving and decisive moment?

WHOSE DREAM ARE YOU FOLLOWING?

1. There are some invisible moments of grace that can take us by surprise. We cannot always name them until they have passed us by. How would you identify that moment in Patrick?

2. How did the spirit of prayer and openness assist Patrick in his discernment?

3. Can you explain why a parental or traditional "dream" may play a huge part in how a young person discerns a life call or future plan of life?

4. What encouraged Patrick to "go forward" in his dream and relinquish the dreams of his family? What price/virtue might someone pay to make this announcement to parents and friends?

5. Can you imagine some issues/points that might hold a person back from making the decision to "follow one's dream?"

A DIVINE PURPOSE

1. How would you answer the question: "What do you want to be when you grow up?"

2. What do you think of the young boy's (in church) response when asked that question?

3. Do we need to understand our vocation before we can be generous in following it?

4. What is the impetus, both immediate and ultimate, to follow one's vocation with generosity?

DO NOT MISS YOUR LIFE

1. What did the rescued Chilean miner promise to God, and what did he mean by that promise?

2. What are the riches of a genuine discernment?

3. Do you ever feel like you are missing your life? If so, elaborate.

4. How should Christians live in the world? (Hint: What does Diognetus suggest?)

5. Does this reflection compel you to adjust your priorities?

LOVE MAKES DEMANDS

1. Sometimes the obstacles we find in discernment may cause us to pause or to stumble. When someone comes into our life and starts modifying our "comfort zones" why may this cause us to stumble? Give an example from your own life.

2. God's plan for our life may come with some costly openness and acceptance. Is there anything in our nature that may cause us "to balk" or resent these changes?

3. What if God's design is in contrast to our own? How do we reconcile the two?

4. All of life's calls, whether marriage, intentional single life, priesthood or religious life, are going to require some restructuring of our current lifestyle, goals, habits, and pleasures. What life changes will be the most challenging for you?

5. What motivates one to radical change? What does one have to allow for? Is this something you resist in your own relationship with the Lord?

LET HOLY DESIRES LEAD

1. What words capture the totality of the spiritual life and why?

2. How do you understand the difference between God's "direct" will and God's "permissive" will? Where have you seen examples of it in your own life?

3. Does our desire for God begin with our initiative?

4. Name the image that reflects St. Catherine of Siena's intimacy with God. Now name your own at this point in your relationship with God. What does that suggest about how you picture God in your life and in your prayer?

5. Where and when do you most experience your desire for God?

INDEX OF SAINTS

St. Catherine of Siena (1347-1380)

One of the greatest mystics and most brilliant theological minds of her time, St. Catherine became a Third Order Dominican at age 18. Her letters of spiritual instruction, direction and encouragement drew many to follow her, lay and ordained. St. Catherine's influence was particularly evident at the time of the Great Schism in 1378 when she famously persuaded Pope Gregory XI to leave Avignon and return the papacy to Rome, hoping to unify the Church, her overarching purpose.

St. Catherine's principal work is a treatise called *The Dialogue*. In 1970, she became the second woman after Teresa of Avila to be named a Doctor of the Church by Pope Paul VI. St. Catherine died when she was only 33, several weeks after her final and famous vision of the Church as a ship resting on her shoulders.

St. Ignatius of Loyola (1491-1556)

Founder of the Society of Jesus, popularly known as the Jesuits, St. Ignatius' greatest work is the "Spiritual Exercises" which he started as a layman. A concentrated blueprint for spiritual examination and discernment, it remains popular today as a highly effective retreat tool. After some years of intense prayer, wandering around looking for a spiritual home, St. Ignatius, with six other companions, resolved to support each other in a communal life centered in poverty, chastity and obedience. Additionally, they professed a forth vow of apostolic service to the Pope. Thus, in 1534, the new Society of Jesus, which was to play such an influential role in the Counter-Reformation, was launched with the motto: *majorem Dei gloriam:* "for the greater glory of God."

Mother Clelia Merloni (1861-1930)

Servant of God Mother Clelia is Foundress of the Apostles of the Sacred Heart of Jesus, an international congregation founded in Italy, whose mission is to spread the love of the Sacred Heart of Jesus in the world. Mother Clelia taught her Sisters to be an "apostle like the first apostles," on mission, leading souls to Christ by making Him known and loved; a "apostle of love," uniting their hearts with the heart of Jesus and the hearts of their Sisters; and an "apostle of reparation," restoring and renewing the Kingdom of God amid the circumstances in which they find themselves.

The Sisters achieve this vision today primarily through the ministry of elementary and secondary education. The motto of their congregation is, *Carita Christi Urget Nos:* "The love of Christ impels us."

St. Angela Merici (1474-1540)
A Third Order Franciscan who founded the Ursuline Order, a secular institute of religious women and the oldest teaching order of women in the Church, St. Angela demonstrated a practical approach to the needs revealed in contemporary society. Her most revolutionary idea for her day and age, was promoting education for all women, including young, unmarried women, beginning with poor girls. She is also known as Angela of Brescia and wrote *Spiritual Testament*.

St. Augustine (354-430)
Bishop of Hippo and a Doctor of the Church, St. Augustine wrote over 93 books. He has 300 letters and 400 sermons credited to him. Is it any wonder that the prolific Augustine has been called one of the greatest minds of Western civilization, one of the foremost Christian apologists, an apostle of the interior life, a prince of mystics, a Christian ascetic and a singularly gifted preacher of polished and creative rhetoric? His unbelievably generous theological, philosophical and spiritual output in such an accessible style of communication is still inexhaustible in its appeal today. One can truly engage his spirituality as personal. He gave exceedingly personal testimony because he shared from a place of tremendous, personal vulnerability. Probably the best-selling book after the Bible, St. Augustine's *Confessions* was written when he was already a Cʳ ʰⁱc for 12 years and a bishop for three. His other famous work is
(₁

˙ (1567-1622)
˙d Bishop of Geneva, St. Francis with St. Jeanne
˙ʳ of the Visitation Nuns. Living in the

religiously divisive times of the Protestant Reformation, St. Francis became popular for his pastoral approach in his homilies, teachings and writings in the areas of spiritual direction and spiritual formation. His principal works are: *Introduction to the Devout Life* and the *Treatise on the Love of God.* He is the patron saint of writers and journalists.

St. Teresa of Avila (1515-1582)
A Carmelite nun and mystic from Spain, St. Teresa is most known as a reformer of the Carmelite Order. Along with St. John of the Cross, she founded the Discalced Carmelites. In 1970, St. Teresa was the first woman to be honored with the title Doctor of the Church for her writings and teachings on prayer. Notable among these are her autobiography as well as *The Way of Perfection* and *The Interior Castle.*

St. Bernadine of Siena (1380-1444)
Known as the Apostle of Italy because of his efforts to revive his country's faith, St. Bernadine can best be described as a tireless Franciscan preacher and missionary for whom devotion to the Holy Name of Jesus was paramount. Through his itinerant preaching across Italy, he was arguably the greatest influence on the popular piety of the people in the fifteenth century. After 12 years as the appointed General Vicar for the Friars of the Strict Observance, he returned to his first love, preaching, until his death.

St. Therese of Lisieux (1873-1897)
Affectionately nicknamed, "The Little Flower," St. Therese was a cloistered Carmelite nun who entered the convent at age 15 only to die at age 24. Thus her spiritual renown and greatness is all the more remarkable. Her only book, her autobiography, became a spiritual masterpiece. Entitled, *Story of a Soul*, it is an edited version of her journal. St. Therese is the patroness of the missions.

St. Clare of Assisi (1194-1253)
One of the first admirers and followers of St. Francis of Assisi, St. Clare founded an order of nuns in the Franciscan spirit now called the "Poor Clares." At age 19, after hearing St. Francis preach, she left home and joined his inspiring cause. St. Francis made her superior at the convent (a

position she held for 40 years) in the Church of San Damiano. Eventually two other sisters and her mother joined her.

St. Thomas Becket (1118-1170)
A martyr, St. Thomas Becket was the Archbishop of Canterbury. When he opposed King Henry II's interference in church matters, hostility grew among the King's knights and he was eventually murdered at the altar in his cathedral by four of them. He is the patron saint of clergy.

St. Aloysius Gonzaga (1568-1591)
Born in Castiglione, Italy, St. Aloysius, like St. Catherine of Siena, knew at an early age that he was called to consecrate his life to God and made a vow of perpetual virginity at age nine. At age 11, he was already instructing poor children on the lessons from the catechism. At age 18, moved by a book on Jesuit missionaries, St. Aloysius entered the Society of Jesus (Jesuits). It was to be a short religious life, but one filled with a decisive example of faith and self-discipline for the sake of the gospel. He died at age 23 as a result of caring for the victims of a plague that struck Rome. St. Aloysius is the patron saint of Catholic youth.

St. Gregory the Great (540-604)
Benedictine monk and Pope, St. Gregory was also known as the "Father of Christian Worship" because of his tireless work revising the Roman worship of his day. Because of his prolific and exceptional achievements and leadership within the violent chaos of the Middle Ages, he became known as Gregory the Great. He is considered one of the top four doctors of the Western Church along with Jerome, Augustine and Ambrose. One of his works that is still highly regarded today is *Pastoral Care*.

St. Thomas Aquinas (1225-1274)
Arguably the greatest and most creative mind Western Civilization has ever produced, St. Thomas Aquinas is a Doctor of the Church and the Father of Classical Thomism. Born four years after St. Dominic's death, he is probably the most famous Dominican after St. Dominic. Raised by the Benedictines, St. Thomas entered the brand new Order of

Preachers despite his family's opposition. They had hoped he would one day assume the prestigious position of abbot at Monte Casino.

As the gifted student of St. Albert the Great, Aquinas' prolific output as a scriptural commentator, philosopher and theologian was unparalleled at the time. Some of his greatest works are: *Commentary on the Gospel of St. John*, *Sermon on the Apostles Creed*, *The Three Greatest Prayers*, *Commentaries on the Commandments and Sacraments (God's Greatest Gifts)*, and *The Compendium of Theology*, a synopsis of his masterpiece, *Summa Theologiae*. A mystic, poet and practical spiritual director, St. Thomas was known by many names reflecting both his academic and spiritual accomplishments. These include: "The Universal Teacher," "The Christian Apostle," and "The Angelic Doctor." He is the patron saint of Catholic Universities.

St. Charles Borromeo (1538-1584)
A Church Reformer in the 16th century, St. Charles was the Cardinal-archbishop of Milan at the time of the Counter-Reformation. His authentic commitment to his faith was demonstrated in achievements as diverse as the formal establishment of the seminary system for the education of priests as well as his care for the victims of the plague in Milan in 1576-77. In his role as papal secretary, he was a key influence in the successful completion of the Council of Trent. His uncle was Pope Pius IV.

St. Romuald (951-1027)
Founder of the Order of Camaldolese Benedictines in Tuscany, St. Romuald was the image personified of the unity possible in living the monastic and hermitical life. After entering monastic life at age 20, he spent three decades founding monasteries and hermitages throughout Italy, at one point welcoming his own father into the monastery as a monk.

St. Margaret Mary Alacoque (1647-1690)
St. Margaret Mary was a religious of the Order of Visitation Nuns. Through her visions of Jesus and Mary, she became a committed apostle of devotion to the Sacred Heart of Jesus. It would not be until 75 years after her death, that devotion to the Sacred Heart would be officially

recognized. She is known as one of the "saints of the Sacred Heart" along with St. John Eudes and her spiritual director, Bl. Claude de la Colimbiere.

St. Ignatius of Antioch (35-107)

A convert to Christianity and Bishop of Antioch, St. Ignatius was known for his teachings and writings on the unity and order of the Church. He was martyred in 107, when the Emperor Trajan visited Antioch and demanded that Christians deny Christ or be killed. On the journey to Rome, the site of his martyrdom, he addressed many inspirational and pastoral letters to Christian communities to whom he would visit and preach.

St. Alphonsus Ligouri (1696-1787)

A Bishop and Doctor of the Church, St. Alphonsus was the founder of the Congregation of the Most Holy Redeemer (Redemptorists), mission preachers who reached out to the rural poor. He was a respected moral theologian, author and preacher whose theology was so well respected as balanced and moderate that it went through 60 editions for over a century after he was gone from the theological scene. St. Alphonsus fought the heresy of Jansenism, an obsessive and scrupulous emphasis on sin and damnation.

St. Alphonsus' primary focus, pastorally, was on the actual day-to-day challenges of pastors and confessors. While best known as a moral theologian, St. Alphonsus also taught in the areas of spiritual and dogmatic theology. He encouraged devotion to the Real Presence through regular visits to the Blessed Sacrament. Popular among his many works is *The Glories of Mary*.

St. Raymond of Peñafort (1180-1275)

A Spanish Dominican friar and canonist in the 13th-century, St. Raymond is known as the patron saint of canon lawyers. His efforts laid the groundwork for a Code of Canon Law. This accomplishment resulted from three years of arduous work compiling several thousand papal and conciliar decrees known as the Decretals of Gregory IX, an influential work in the area of Church law right into the 20th century. St. Raymond was elected third Master of the Dominican Order in 1238. His other principle work was *Summa de casibus poenitentiae* (A Synthesis of Cases Related to the Sacrament of Penance).

St. Basil the Great (329-379)
Archbishop of Caesarea, St. Basil was one of the most influential theologians and gifted orators among the early Church Fathers. He successfully led the ongoing battle against Arianism. Additionally, he fought against simony (the buying and selling of ecclesiastical offices) and promoted a strict reform of the clergy. His personal holiness was evident in the shepherd's care he gave to the drought and famine victims of his time. Having likely founded the first monastery in Asia Minor, he remains an abiding and prominent presence within Eastern monasticism today.

St. Braulio (590-651)
Bishop of Zaragoza (having succeeded his brother, Bishop John of Zaragoza), St. Braulio battled the last vestiges of the Arian heresy. He was a gifted scholar and compelling preacher who touched many with his example of committed asceticism, pastoral care, and generosity to the poor.

St. Joseph Cafasso (1811-1860)
A Catholic priest, sought-after-preacher and social reformer in 19th century Turin, St. Joseph, was known as one of the "Social Saints of the City" at that time, earning that designation primarily though his work with prisoners and the inhumane conditions in which they lived. A popular spiritual director, confessor and lecturer (primarily in moral theology), he was the ultimate influence on John Bosco, founder of the Salesians, to pursue a vocation in the education of young boys. He also fought rigorously against the spread of Jansenism.

St. Phillip Neri (1515-1595)
A priest and popular confessor, St. Philip was the founder of the Oratory, a religious institute of priests who lived together in community. His personal example of holiness and humility, within a cheerful and jocular disposition, made him an attractive, prominent figure of the Counter-

Reformation. Three centuries later, Cardinal Newman would found the first English-speaking house of the Oratory.

St. Isidore of Seville (560-636)

A lover of learning, St. Isidore was nicknamed "The Schoolmaster of the Middle Ages." He strongly recommended that a seminary be established throughout the dioceses of Spain and made sure that all branches of knowledge, including the arts and medicine, were taught in the schools he founded. His principal work was *The Etymologies*, an encyclopedia of knowledge that maintained its influence in the popular imagination for almost a millennium. Other works include a dictionary, a history of the Goths, a history of the world and his *Book of Maxims*.

GLOSSARY OF TERMS

Ad Sum
Latin expression which means "I am here."

Alter Christus
A Latin term which means "Other Christ."

Call
The specific invitation to serve God in religious life, priesthood, married life or the intentional single life.

Celibacy
The renunciation of marriage made by those who receive the sacrament of Holy Orders and are called to a more perfect observance of chastity "for the sake of the kingdom."

Chastity
The vow of chastity commits a person to refrain from voluntary sexual pleasure, whether interior or exterior: thus its object is identical with what the virtue of chastity imposes outside the marriage state. A classically spiritual understanding of chastity is "an undivided heart."

Come & See Visit
A popular title for the part of the process of discerning a call which entails visiting a specific congregation, religious order, institute or seminary.

Commitment
The full and permanent giving of one's whole self faithfully to religious life and/or priesthood through God's grace has long had its place in classical Catholic tradition.

Consolation
A common term in spiritual discernment that refers to the experience of interior affirmation and assurance of the direction one is seeking to go. Its exterior effect is to free one from a preoccupation with self and help a person to recognize and more fully appreciate the joys and sorrows of

others. It positively directs a person's focus outside and beyond him/herself.

Contemplative Prayer
Prayer said with the "attention of the mind centered at the heart" where words are not verbally spoken. It consists of sitting completely still in loving awareness of God's presence. In this prayer, the soul is fixed solely on God without the use of images, meditative thoughts or verbal petitions. To help still the mind, a simple one or two syllable word is used or the method of simply following one's rhythmic breathing.

Discernment
Is a multi-step process of coming to understand how the Lord is inviting one to serve Him; a person seeks to discover God's presence and action in her/his life and acts on it concretely.

Desolation
The opposite of consolation, this term refers to an interior experience of darkness and anxiety that has a person negatively turning in on him/herself. Its external effect is to be continually discouraged and despairing about things one use to be engaged in with great hope and satisfaction.

Formation
The multi-year period of preparation for the consecrated life or priesthood.

Lumen Gentium
Latin term meaning "Light of the Nations." It is the title of one of the principle documents to come out of the Roman Catholic Church's Second Vatican Council.

Obedience
In the vow of obedience, a person strives to live a life in a stance of listening and responding to God's will rather than fostering one's own.

Perfecta Caritatis
A document of Vatican II which defines the adaptation and renewal of religious life proclaimed by Pope Paul VI.

Poverty
The vow of poverty professed by religious is a radical call to freedom and apostolic availability. Unrestricted by the accumulation of wealth and material possessions, people are free to focus on relationships and service for the sake of the Kingdom of God.

Stages of Vocation Discernment:
Five stages (in this book) that describe the pathway to discovering God's will for one's life.

Sanctity
Holiness or sanctity is the outcome of sanctification, that Divine act by which God purifies the soul by virtue and good works, thereby making one holy.

Unum Necessarium
The Latin term for the ***One Thing Necessary*** which refers to union with God as the most important thing a Christian should be about whatever the task at hand.

Vita Consecrata
A Latin expression meaning the "Consecrated Life." It refers to the well-known document by Saint John Paul II on religious life and its many rich dimensions.

Vocation
Rooted in the Latin word *vocare*, which means "call," it refers to a specifically recognized way within the Church of serving God either though the priesthood, consecrated life, intentional single life or married life.